j411 Jef

Transportation & Communication Series

All About Braille
Reading By Touch

Laura S. Jeffrey

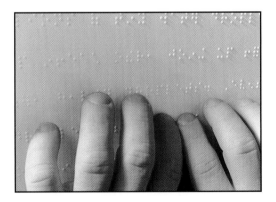

Enslow Publishers, Inc.

40 Industrial Road	PO Box 38
Box 398	Aldershot
Berkeley Heights, NJ 07922	Hants GU12 6BP
USA	UK

http://www.enslow.com

Library of Congress Cataloging-in-Publication Data

Jeffrey, Laura S.
    All about Braille : reading by touch / Laura S. Jeffrey.
      v. cm. — (Transportation & communication series)
    Includes bibliographical references and index.
    Contents: A girl named Helen—Finger reading—Changing a secret code
—Communicating and getting around—From teachers to musicians—
Braille for today and tomorrow.
    ISBN 0-7660-2184-X
    1. Braille—Juvenile literature. 2. People with visual
disabilities—Juvenile literature. 3. Braille, Louis,
1809–1852—Juvenile literature. [1. Braille. 2. Blind. 3. People with
visual disabilities. 4. Braille, Louis, 1809–1852.] I. Title. II. Series.
HV1672.J44 2004
411—dc22
                              2003017617

Printed in the United States of America

10 9 8 7 6 5 4 3 2 1

To Our Readers: We have done our best to make sure all Internet Addresses in this book were active and appropriate when we went to press. However, the author and the publisher have no control over and assume no liability for the material available on those Internet sites or on other Web sites they may link to. Any comments or suggestions can be sent by e-mail to comments@enslow.com or to the address on the back cover.

Every effort has been made to locate all copyright holders of material used in this book. If any errors or omissions have occurred, corrections will be made in future editions of this book.

Illustration Credits: Courtesy of the American Action Fund for Blind Children and Adults, p. 12; AP Photos, p. 20; © 1996-2003 ArtToday.com, Inc., pp. 2, 11, 23, 29; Associated Press, p. 28 (all); Associated Press, US MINT, p. 9; Courtesy of the Braille Bug Web site from the American Foundation for the Blind, p. 37; Photos courtesy of Braille Institute/Jim Rush, pp. 34, 36; Collection of the Callahan Museum of the American Printing House for the Blind, pp. 16, 22 (top); © Corel Corporation, p. 29; Courtesy of Enabling Technologies, p. 25; Enslow Publishers, Inc., pp. 19 (recreation of Charles Barbier's night writing), 39; Courtesy of Freedom Scientific, pp. 22 (bottom), 24; Hemera Technologies, Inc. 1997-2000, p. 18; © Didrick Johnck /Corbis Sygma, pp. 30, 31; Parks Canada/Alexander Graham Bell National Historic Site of Canada, p. 6; Photos Courtesy of Perkins School for the Blind, pp. 1, 4, 5, 7, 8, 10, 21, 33, 38; Photo courtesy of The Seeing Eye, pp. 26, 27; Photo courtesy of U.S. Department of Labor, p. 32.

Cover Illustration: Photo Courtesy of Perkins School for the Blind.

Contents

4 ⚃ ⚄

A Girl Named Helen

Helen Keller became sick as a child and was left blind and deaf.

More than one hundred twenty years ago, a baby girl was born in Alabama. Her name was Helen Keller. When she was almost two years old, she became very ill. Keller got better, but the illness left her blind and deaf.

Keller could not see, and she could not hear. Her parents were very worried. What kind of life would this child have? Soon, though, Keller showed that she was a very special person. By the time she was eight years old, she was famous. She was pen pals with Alexander Graham Bell, the inventor of the telephone. When she was twenty years old, Helen Keller went to college. She was the first blind-deaf

Keller (left) sits and reads Braille.

Helen Keller was pen pals with Alexander Graham Bell. Here he is with Keller and Anne Sullivan (standing).

person ever to go to college.

Helen Keller was a writer. She wrote poems and magazine articles. She wrote about her life in an autobiography called *The Story of My Life*. She wrote other books, too. Keller also went all over the world. She met many important people. She even met United States presidents. In 1964, President Lyndon B. Johnson gave Keller the Presidential Medal of Freedom.

This was a very important honor for Keller. The Presidential Medal of Freedom is given to people who do great things to help others. It is the highest honor that is given to people not in the military.

Keller also received many other awards.

Movies were made about her life. Keller even starred in one of these movies. She gave speeches and helped to raise money for groups helping blind people. She worked to get laws passed. Many people thought blind and deaf people were helpless. Keller showed them they were wrong.

When Helen Keller died in June 1968, at the age of eighty-seven, she had done many great things. How did Keller do so much? She had a teacher named Anne Sullivan. Sullivan came to live with Keller when Keller was a little girl. She taught Keller by spelling words in her hand. She was with Keller all the time. She stayed with

Anne Sullivan taught Keller how to finger spell and read Braille.

Helen Keller did a lot of great things in her life, including learning to read and write Braille.

Keller until they were both old women. (Anne Sullivan died in 1936, when Keller was fifty-six years old.) Through Sullivan, the world opened up to Keller.

Keller also did well because she could read and write. To do these things, she used Braille.

Braille helped Keller read books. It also helped her learn what other people felt and believed.

In later years, as Anne Sullivan grew older, she herself became blind. It was then that Keller taught Braille to Sullivan. Braille had changed in the many years since Sullivan first taught it to Keller. Keller wanted to help her teacher learn so that she, too, could enjoy reading and writing again. Helen Keller wanted to give Anne Sullivan an important gift. That gift was Braille.

Helen Keller is pictured on the Alabama quarter. Notice the Braille above her name.

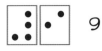

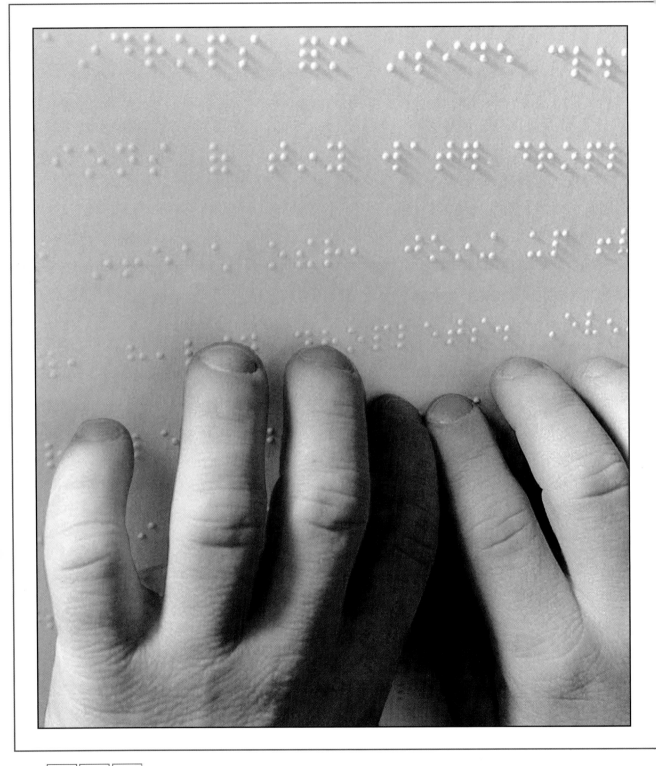

10

Finger Reading

Most people learn to read by looking at the letters of the alphabet. They learn each letter by its shape. They learn which sounds each letter makes. Then they learn how to put together letters to form words.

Blind people are not able to see letters, but they can still read. Instead of seeing letters, they feel them. They do this by using Braille. Braille is a reading system. It uses raised dots that blind people can feel. These dots are grouped in different ways. Each group of dots stands for a letter of the alphabet, a number, a punctuation mark, or a special symbol. Blind people feel the dots with their fingertips. They

People who are blind or visually impaired can read Braille with their finger tips (left).

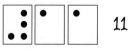

11

memorize the different shapes and what the shapes represent. That is why Braille is also called finger reading.

Each group of Braille dots is called a cell. Each cell contains up to six dots. Here is an example of a Braille cell. This cell is "full" because there are dots by every number.

The letter *a* is made in Braille by one dot after Number 1. The letter *b* is formed by two dots, one after Number 1 and the other after Number 2. Look at the Braille alphabet on page 13. Can you write your name using Braille?

Braille has cells for each letter of the alphabet. It also has cells for numbers, capital letters, punctuation marks, and even musical notes. Braille also has cells for contractions.

A contraction is a short word that stands for two words. For example, "isn't" is a contraction for "is not." Braille includes cells for these

The American Action Fund For Blind Children and Adults publishes books in Braille for children and adults.

12

common contractions. It also has contractions for words that are used a lot, such as "and" and "the."

Look at the Braille alphabet below. To write the word "the," you could use three cells.

Try to write your name in Braille.

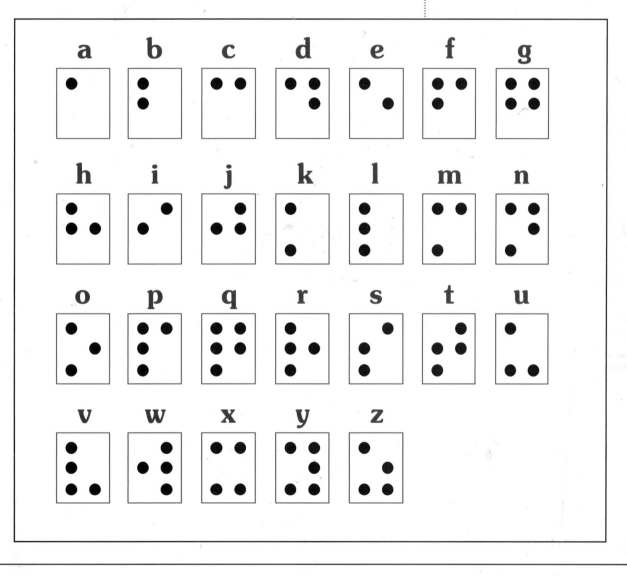

13

Two ways for the word "the" in Braille:

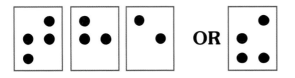

Capital letters in Braille have a special dot before the letter. This dot tells readers that the word they are about to read should be capitalized, like the name of a person.

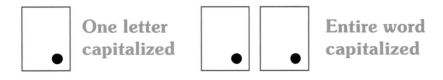

Braille numbers use the same dots as letters *a* through *j*. Before each number there is a special sign letting readers know they are reading a number.

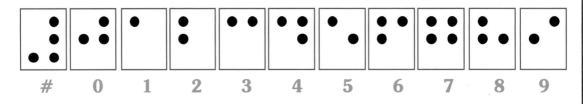

| # | 0 | 1 | 2 | 3 | 4 | 5 | 6 | 7 | 8 | 9 |

Here is some punctuation in Braille:

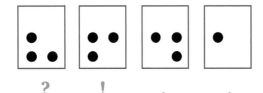

? ! . ,

The first cell is for the letter *t*. The second cell is for the letter *h*. The third cell is for the letter *e*. Or, you could use the Braille contraction for *the*. It is only one cell.

Braille also has short ways to write long words. For example, *tm* is used for tomorrow, and *ll* is used for "little." There are about 180 contractions in Braille. These contractions help to save space. Otherwise, Braille books would be very, very long.

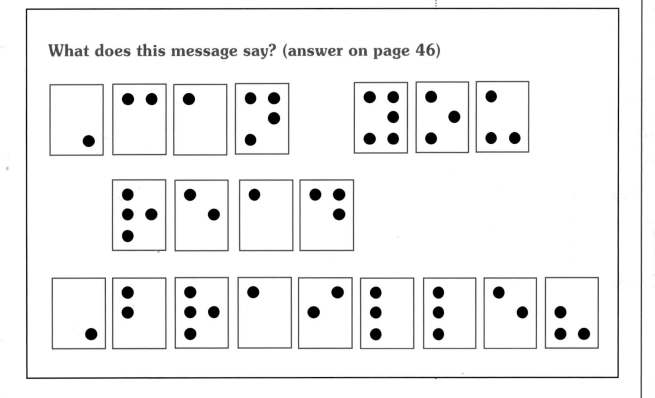

What does this message say? (answer on page 46)

15

Chapter 3

Changing a Secret Code

When Louis Braille lived in Paris, there were beautiful streets and houses.

Braille is named after the person who invented it. Louis Braille was born in 1809 in a town near Paris, France. He could see when he was born. When he was three years old, he had a terrible accident. One day, he went to his father's workshop and played with the tools. He poked himself in the eye with a very sharp tool. His mother put a bandage on the eye, but his eye became infected. The infection spread, and Louis became blind.

When he was old enough, Louis went to school. He was the only blind student. He learned by listening to the teachers. When Louis was ten, he was sent to a special school

When Louis Braille (left) was three years old, he poked himself in the eye with a sharp tool. His eyes became infected and he lost his sight. At fifteen, he made a reading system of raised dots that he called Braille.

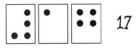

for blind children. It was called the Royal Institution for Blind Youth. Now it is called the National Institution for Blind Youth. It is in Paris. This school had some books for blind children to read. The books had words written in large capital letters. The letters were raised so that the students could feel them and then put them together to figure out the words. This system was hard for the blind children. It took them a long time to learn how to read this way.

Louis read these books, but he thought he could figure out a better way to make books for blind people. Louis began to think about a code that could be used for each letter of the alphabet.

One day when Louis was twelve, a soldier visited the school. The soldier's name was Charles Barbier. He told Louis and the other

Louis could not read the textbooks at school, so he listened to the teachers instead.

students about his invention called night writing. Night writing used raised dots and dashes to represent words. The soldiers could read messages by tracing the dots and dashes with their fingers. They used this system to talk to each other in the dark and without speaking. Enemy soldiers could not hear them.

Louis was happy to learn about night writing. He thought he could change it to make a writing code for blind people. Night writing used twelve dots to form letters. Louis changed that number to six. He thought six was the most dots people could touch with one fingertip. Louis worked hard on his system. At fifteen years old, after many tries, he created a dot code. He showed this code to the principal of his school. He called his system Braille. In 1829, when Louis was twenty years old, he published the first Braille book.

Louis also liked math and music. He made Braille for numbers and music. Louis became a

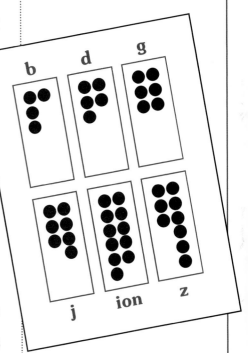

The night writing (above) used by soldier Charles Barbier gave Louis Braille an idea. He could use it to help blind people read and write.

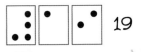

teacher at the Royal Institution for Blind Youth. He taught others his code.

For many years, Braille was not used everywhere. Many people tried to make other codes to help blind people to read. But soon, Louis Braille's system was thought to be the best.

Because of Louis Braille's invention, blind and visually impaired people all over the world today can write. They can also read their favorite books.

Today, blind people all over the world use Braille to read. They can figure out math problems and create music. Thanks to Braille, words, numbers, and musical notes are no longer just something people see. They are also things people can feel.

People can also write Braille by using special tools, like this Braillewriter, or Brailler.

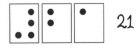

Chapter 4

Communicating and Getting Around

A slate and stylus are important tools for Braille writing. A slate is made of two pieces of metal or plastic. They are attached by a hinge at one end. The other end opens up to hold a piece of paper. At the top of the slate are rows of Braille cells. A stylus is a pointed piece of metal. It is used to punch through the Braille cells. The Braille dots are then embossed on the piece of paper. A slate and stylus can be any size. One size can be used to write on postcards or small sheets of paper.

Braillewriters work like typewriters. They have six keys, one for each dot in a Braille cell. Blind people type using the six keys. When a

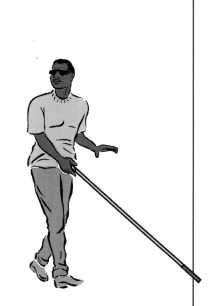

Blind and visually impaired people might use special canes to help them find their way around.

There are many tools that blind and visually impaired people can use to write Braille. This washboard slate (top left) is one of them. Braille displays (bottom left) let people use their computers. They can read and send email using these Braille displays.

key is struck, the Braille dot is embossed on the piece of paper in the Braillewriter.

Another useful tool is a Braille display. It attaches to a computer. It helps people who read and write Braille send and receive computer messages in Braille.

Some blind people use Braille note takers. They are like handheld computers. They have a Braille keyboard that is like keys on the Braillewriter. Blind people can use them to make notes. The notes are stored in the computer. These notes can be read with a built-in Braille display. Or, a computerized voice reads aloud what has been written.

Note takers are handheld computers that let people take notes using Braille. Note takers can talk to the person as they are surfing the Internet or working.

Students like to use these portable Braille computers to take notes in school or send email.

24

Braille printers are also called embossers. They work like computer printers. But instead of printing words, they emboss Braille dots onto paper. Blind people can use these printers to make hard copies of computer files in Braille.

Some children's books have pages with both words and Braille. That is so blind people and sighted people can read aloud together.

These are all tools for using Braille. There are other kinds of tools that help people. Video description is a way for blind people to enjoy television programs and videotapes. A voice describes what is happening during the program. Some telephones are made for blind people who also cannot hear. Instead of picking up the phone and listening to the caller, the person receives the message as electronic pulses. These pulses move pins to become

Braille printers are also called embossers. They print the raised dots on both sides of the paper at the same time.

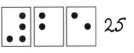

 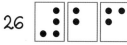

Braille dots on a Braille display. They feel the Braille words with their fingertips.

In the 1920s, a woman named Dorothy Eustis began training German shepherds to help blind people get around. Now, all kinds of dogs are trained as guide dogs. Guide dogs are specially-trained dogs. Not all dogs can be guide dogs. The dogs have to be very smart and willing to work hard.

Some people use a special white cane to help them get around. The white cane also lets other people know that a person is blind.

Guide dogs learn to help their owners cross busy streets (left). This woman is training the dog to be a guide dog.

Guide dogs are very important. They help blind and visually impaired people get around by themselves. Guide dogs have to be trained in a special way. This dog is learning how to lead the man onto the bus.

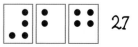

Ray Charles

Claude Monet

Stevie Wonder

28

Chapter 5

From Teachers to Musicians

This is Monet's "Field of Poppies." Even though Monet became blind as he got older, he still painted.

People who are visually impaired or blind can do almost anything. They can be teachers, scientists, business owners, and lawmakers. Claude Monet, a famous French painter, became blind as he grew older. He still created art. So did Edgar Degas, a French painter and sculptor. President Theodore Roosevelt was partially blind. He was also partially deaf.

Famous blind musicians include Ray Charles, Ronnie Milsap, and Sonny Terry. Stevie Wonder is another famous blind musician. He is a singer, songwriter, musician, and producer. Wonder went blind as a newborn baby. He showed musical talent at

Visually impaired and blind people can do almost anything. Claude Monet was a famous French painter who continued to paint after he became blind. Ray Charles is a famous musician. Stevie Wonder has won many awards for his music.

a very early age. By the time he was twelve years old, he had released his first record. Wonder has won awards for his music. He is also respected for the causes he supports. He wrote a song to persuade lawmakers to make Martin Luther King, Jr.'s birthday a national holiday. He has written songs to help end world hunger.

Robert Smithdas and his wife, Michelle, are both blind and deaf. They were married in 1975. Robert became blind at the age of five and deaf at the age of twelve. He was a swimmer and a wrestler. He became the second blind-deaf person, after Helen Keller, to graduate from college. In 1953, Robert earned his master's degree. He was the first blind-deaf person to earn an advanced degree.

Michelle Smithdas, Robert's wife, also earned a master's degree. Both Robert and Michelle work at the Helen Keller National Center in New York.

Through all kinds of weather and over ice, Erik Weihenmayer climbs to the top. Read about him on the next page.

Climbing to the Top

There are mountains that only about a hundred people can say they have climbed. These mountains are the tallest on each of the seven continents. Together they are called the "seven summits." It takes skill, strength, endurance, and hard work to climb these mountains.

The Seven Summits
Mount Everest (Nepal, Asia), 29,028 feet
Aconcagua (Argentina, South America), 22,834 feet
Mount McKinley (Alaska, North America), 20,320 feet
Mount Kilimanjaro (Tanzania, Africa), 19,341 feet
Mount Elbrus (Russia, Europe), 18,510 feet
Vinson Massif (Sentinel Range, Antarctica), 16,066 feet
Mount Kosciusko (New South Wales, Australia), 7,310 feet

Erik Weihenmayer has climbed each of the seven mountains. He is a mountain climber who also is blind. Weihenmayer carries his own gear, sets up tents, builds snow walls, and climbs using trekking poles. He travels with a team of other climbers. The climber in front of him wears bells so Weihenmayer can follow the sound. He uses his trekking poles to find trails in the snow.

After losing his sight from a rare eye disease at the age of thirteen, Weihenmayer at first struggled with his blindness. But then, instead of focusing on things he could not do, he focused on the things he could do. In high school in Connecticut, he was the second-ranked wrestler in his weight class. Weihenmayer also bikes, runs, and skydives.

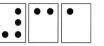

Roy Grizzard works in the United States government to help disabled people. President George W. Bush appointed Grizzard to this job in 2002. Grizzard used to be a teacher and assistant principal. When he was forty years old, he was declared legally blind. He continued to work in schools before going to work for the government. Today, he lives in Ashland, Virginia. He rides the train to his job

Roy Grizzard (left) is the first Assistant Secretary for Disability Employment Policy.

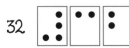

in Washington, D.C. During the workweek, he lives by himself in an apartment in Arlington, Virginia.

Blind people can do almost any kind of work, but they may need special training. They also may need equipment, such as Braillewriters and Braille displays. Several organizations help blind people get job training and find jobs. These organizations also help people learn Braille. Braille is very important to learn. Braille will help blind children do well in school and as adults.

Children all over the world can learn to read and write Braille.

The organizations also want to teach Braille to people who can see. Then people can become Braille teachers. Or, they will be better prepared if they ever lose their sight. Many people that are now blind were born with sight. They became blind later on in life.

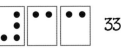

Chapter 6

Today and Tomorrow

French teenager Louis Braille invented a very important code. Yet today, many blind children do not learn Braille. The number of blind children who know Braille has gone down in the past forty years. One study found that only one in ten blind children knows Braille.

Groups that help blind people know that if blind children do not learn Braille, they may not learn to read or write. They may not be able to live by themselves. They are less likely to be able to find a good-paying job.

One group that helps blind people is the Braille Institute in San Diego, California. In June 2003, the Braille Institute held the third

The Braille Challenge shows just how important Braille is to learn. People who compete are tested in different events. In this event (left), people listen to headphones and type, in Braille, what they hear.

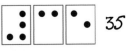

During the Braille Challenge, children compete in different events. In this event, spelling correctly is important.

Another event at the Braille Challenge includes reading a passage and then answering questions.

 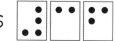

annual Braille Challenge. The Braille Institute holds the Braille Challenge every year. The Braille Challenge is a contest for children who read and write Braille. Children ages six to nineteen come from all over the United States to California. They compete in Braille reading, spelling, proofreading, and word searches.

The American Foundation for the Blind created a Web site called the Braille Bug.

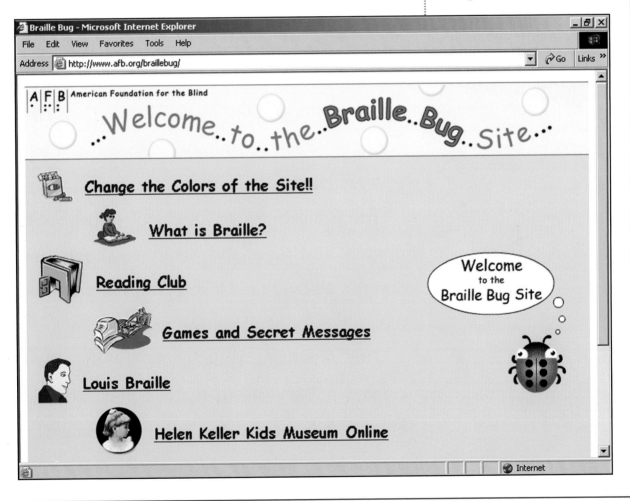

There are many people who are blind or have trouble seeing. Braille is just one way that lets them communicate with others.

Braille helps children and adults in their lives. These young adults are learning to use their Braillewriters.

They win prizes. The Braille Institute hopes the contest will encourage blind children everywhere to learn and practice Braille.

The Braille Institute also helps to get books printed in Braille and sent to schools and libraries all over the United States. It publishes magazines for blind people, too.

The American Foundation for the Blind created a Web site to teach sighted children about Braille. It is called the Braille Bug. This group also has an information packet for sighted children about Braille reading, writing, and math. It is called the Braille Trail.

The Louis Braille Center created the Braille Workbox. This is a collection of study sheets about Braille for older children. There are also many books to help people. The *Braille Connection* is one of these books. It helps teach older students and adults who have lost their sight how to use Braille.

Braille is an important first step in helping blind people. There are other ways to help. Money helps to educate Braille teachers. It buys tools for blind people to use in schools, homes, and offices. In 1990, lawmakers passed the Americans with Disabilities Act. This law says public places have to be accessible for people with blindness and other disabilities.

Jobs for blind people are also needed. Many groups teach employers about the kinds of jobs that blind people can do, and the training and equipment they need to be good workers. They also publish directories so that blind

Braille can be found in many places, such as near elevator buttons. See if you can find other places that use Braille.

You can send a friend a card written in Braille.

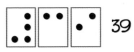

people and their families know where they can get help.

Today, about 10 million Americans are either blind or have a very hard time seeing. People can be born blind, or they can develop blindness later in life. Braille helps these people lead happy productive lives.

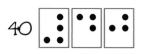

Timeline

1809—Louis Braille is born; loses his sight at three years old from an infection.

1824—Louis Braille develops a reading system of raised dots, called Braille.

1829—Louis Braille publishes the first book in Braille.

1880—Helen Keller is born; loses her sight at around two years old from an illness.

Late 1890s—First Braillewriter is made.

1902—Helen Keller writes *The Story of My Life*.

1920s—Dorothy Eustis begins training German shepherds to help blind people get around.

1951—The Perkins Brailler is designed and is used today in schools and for general use.

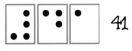

Timeline

1984—Stevie Wonder wins an Academy Award for his song, "I Just Called to Say I Love You."

1990—Lawmakers pass the Americans with Disabilities Act.

1994—NFB-Newsline for the blind is developed to make newspapers accessible over the telephone to blind and visually impaired people.

1997—Congress passes the Amendment to Individuals with Disabilities Education Act (IDEA) to make Braille instruction available to all blind students who want it.

Today—People can use many different devices to read and write Braille. They can use a slate and stylus, a Brailler, or an electronic device.

 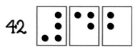

Words to Know

Academy Award—The Academy Award, also called an Oscar, is the main film award in the United States.

accessible—Having the ability of being reached or used. For example, the hotel is accessible by train. You can reach the hotel by train.

autobiography—The story of a person's life written by that person.

blind—Not being able to see.

deaf—Not being able to hear.

directory—A list that is in alphabetical order. A telephone book is a directory.

emboss—To make a raised pattern or design.

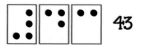

Words to Know

encourage—To give courage or hope.

endurance—Being able to put up with hardship or strain.

infection—Any sickness caused by germs.

require—To have a need for something.

typewriter—A machine that prints letters and other figures when keys are pushed down.

visually impaired—Having a hard time seeing.

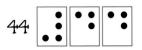

Learn More About
Braille

Books

Collins, S. Harold. *Braille for the Sighted*. New York: Garlic Press, 1998.

Freedman, Russell. *Out of Darkness: The Story of Louis Braille*. Boston, Mass.: Houghton Mifflin Company, 1999.

Jensen, Virginia Allen. *Red Thread Riddles*. New York: Penguin Putnam Books for Young Readers, 1983. (With text in Braille and Standard Type)

Newth, Philip. *Roly Goes Exploring*. New York: Penguin Putnam Books for Young Readers, 1987. (With text in Braille and Standard Type)

Videos

Jake and the Secret Code. Baltimore, Maryland: National Federation of the Blind, 2000.

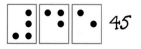

Learn Even More

Internet Addresses

How Vision Works

<http://science.howstuffworks.com/eye.htm>

Learn how the eye works.

National Braille Press

<http://www.nbp.org>

Click on "The Braille alphabet" to open a page where you can type in your name and then see it in Braille.

Questions from Kids About Blindness

<http://www.nfb.org/kids.htm>

This link from the National Federation of the Blind (NFB) answers many questions from kids about who? what? where? how? will? do? and should?

You've Got Braille

<http://pbskids.org/arthur/print/braille/braille_guide.html>

Check out "Marina's Guide to Braille and More."

Answer to message on page 15: Can you read Braille?

Index

Index